When it comes to man projects, is your organization in complete disarray?

Or is everyone flying in the same direction?

THE V-FORMATION METHOD™

Universal Project Management System

Fly Your Organization to the Rapid and Successful
Planning, Management and Completion of its
Projects and the Attainment of its Goals...by
Incorporating the Lessons of Migratory Birds

Bob Bendis and Don Corsaro
Visionary Business Life and Leadership Coaches

Lonely-at-the-Top Publications
Cleveland, Ohio

ISBN: 978-0615468334

Lonely-at-the-Top Publications books are available at special quantity discounts for use in sales promotions, as employee premiums, for educational purposes, or for corporate training programs. Please contact our Special Sales department at: sales@v-formationmethod.com

For Additional Help or to Provide Feedback, contact authors by email at: flightcoach@v-formationmethod.com

The Goose With the Golden Egg

ONE day a countryman going to the nest of his Goose found there an egg all yellow and glittering. When he took it up it was as heavy as lead and he was going to throw it away, because he thought a trick had been played upon him. But he took it home on second thoughts, and soon found to his delight that it was an egg of pure gold. Every morning the same thing occurred, and he soon became rich by selling his eggs. As he grew rich he grew greedy; and thinking to get at once all the gold the Goose could give, he killed it and opened it only to find....nothing.

"GREED OFT O'ERREACHES ITSELF"

Aesop Fable
- -

"It is a fact that in the right formation, the lifting power of many wings can achieve twice the distance of any bird flying alone."

Author Unknown
- -

"Put on YOUR mask first and THEN help those around you who need assistance."

Airline Pre-Takeoff Safety Instruction:

A PERFECT PROJECT "VISION STATEMENT"

"I believe that this nation should commit itself to achieving the goal, before this decade is out, of landing a man on the moon and returning him safely to the earth"

John F. Kennedy
Address to Congress
May 25, 1961

PREFACE

Perhaps no other event is more disruptive and damaging to organization morale and to otherwise smooth-running daily operations than the introduction of "a project".

In our decades of business coaching and consulting and our prior lives as senior executives, we witnessed this phenomenon time and time again.

Picture this scenario: someone in an organization decides a problem needs to be solved or something needs to be done better or faster or cheaper. Perhaps a new system or a new strategy is needed. Or perhaps new methods need to be explored. So, what does this person do? He/she suggests the creation of a "project".

What does every project need? It needs:
a. a mission
b. a project manager and planning team members
c. a process
d. a time frame and budget
e. resources.

(What it REALLY needs, but seldom gets, is significant, top level management support.)

The issues are immediate and numerous:
a. Every Project Manager has a unique management "style", or no managing experience and, therefore, no known "style" at all ... so team members do not know what to expect.

b. Project Managers who are junior to upper management may be unable to demand time and resources needed for their project, let alone management time to report progress, nor priority status versus regular day-to-day activities.

c. With no uniform project management systems and processes in place, such tools need to be devised for each new project, wasting time and resources and, offering no uniformity.

d. Receiving no status and no rewards makes membership on a project team an unattractive prospect and, not uncommonly, a career-threatening activity

The team members and, often, the project manager are torn from their normal daily duties to serve on the project team. They may bring a diversity of skills to the team, but they may never have worked together before and may have no "team" affinity to each other or to the project manager; and the project manager may never have "managed" before. Even harder, the project manager may be junior in corporate ranking to others on the team, or may report to project sponsor who lacks the ear of needed senior decision makers. Styles clash. Fear and frustration abound. Commitment to the project is difficult. What effect will this project have on the members' "regular" jobs? Will those positions even still be available when the project ends. (After all, someone needs to perform the job activity while the project members are working on the "project".)

Data and results of the project have no permanent home, no place to be filed, no way to be accessed in the future. So, the next time a "project" is launched, the organization has to start all over again from scratch.

The psychological and physical disruption to organization operation can be devastating. And while this disruption is going on, the project team will be disheartened and the project may well fail as a result.

Over the longer term, relationships among co-workers may be permanently and irreparably damaged. Some good people may be lost.

Our challenge was how to make "projects" in any organization fun, non-threatening, meaningful, replicable and successful... and provide a template for data gathering and maintenance and for future project activities.

Our solution is the subject of this book...and of **THE V-FORMATION METHOD™ PROGRAM.**

Our motivation was the power, majesty, efficiency and productivity of migratory birds.

TABLE OF CONTENTS

PART II: <u>The V-Formation Method</u>™   61
System in Action
A manufacturer addresses an issue

INTRODUCTION

The "Science" of Migratory Birds

Is there anything more majestic, mystifying and inspiring than the sight of a flight of migrating birds flying in "V" Formation?

"Science" is enclosed in quotation marks simply because birds can't talk, so we can only theorize how and why they do the things they do by observing their behavior. Nevertheless, observation of their migrating behavior is not only scientifically enlightening, but sociologically and culturally instructive as well.

Studies of migrating geese flying in "V" formation have provided the following significant observations for our purposes:

1. The flight leader clearly knows the flight's intended destination and is tasked to be sure that every action of the echelon (or "wedge" or "v") is movement toward the destination.

2. When the flight leader tires, it falls back to the middle of one of the echelon's wings and another bird, obviously qualified to lead the flight, moves up to take its place.

3. Each bird is provided uplift by the bird in front of it, allowing the echelon to increase distances traveled without stopping to rest by seventy percent or more over the distance each bird could have achieved on its own.

4. The birds at the rear of each wing also tire and are observed moving forward to the middle of the wings to rest.

5. Birds to the rear are heard to honk continuous encouragement to the birds ahead of them.

6. If a bird falls from formation, two other birds go with it and stay with it until it either recovers or can't go on.

They then join a formation until they can find and re-join their own formation.

7. "V" formation allows each bird to have the maximum visual awareness of the other birds, their flight direction and of its surroundings.

(One of the most practical applications of these learnings can be observed in the actions and formations of military aircraft which clearly are designed to emulate migration behavior.)

What amazing structure and organization and purpose! How can we apply this "v formation" behavior to the issues that "projects" cause organizations? How do we relate the two?

Project Management and <u>The V-Formation Method</u>™

Exactly what is a **"project"**? Wikipedia provided a simple definition. It tells us that "a **<u>project</u>** is a <u>temporary</u> endeavor, having a defined beginning and end...undertaken to meet unique goals and objectives, usually to bring about beneficial change or added value."

Because a "project" is both <u>temporary</u> and <u>defined by its specific goals</u>, it commonly is required to function within the strict limitations of fixed constraints such as allocated time, budget and resources.

Unlike the management of normal, ongoing business functions, project management must deal with the challenge of having to direct a diversity of staff to the accomplishment of the specific goals of the project, all within the bounds of its constraints. And longer projects may be further disrupted by personnel changes.

"Project Management" certainly has evolved over time. More status is now given to professional Project Managers. Enterprises have created "PMO's" (Project Management Offices) to try to ensure that all projects are created and approved uniformly. But many of the same conflicts still exist. Multiple projects within an enterprise breed competitive pressures as project managers and teams vie for management attention and access to limited resources, tools, facilities and skilled personnel. And, again, multiple projects with multiple managers, with differing management styles and different interpretations of project goals, inevitably result in confusion, competition, turmoil and conflict. And all of this is in addition to the fears, angers, insecurities and confusions we noted above in the **Preface**.

We wondered if there might not be a way to introduce a single, universal project management "system" that could be used by any type of group or enterprise of any size and one that would offer consistent and uniform:

Infrastructure

Structure and Systems

Processes and Procedures

Terminology

Reporting and Measurements

Easily Maintained and Accessible Records and Templates

Rewards

AND…. would replace FRUSTRATION with FUN.

A system that would provide uniformity of methods, easy replication, and an emphasis on teamwork.

A system that would work for any type of project as well as at every level from a single small group to a large international organization.

Then, one day, the answer appeared over our heads....a flight of migrating birds crossing paths with a flight of military aircraft. And so...we developed **The V-Formation Method™**. (It didn't exactly happen that way, of course, but this does sound rather dramatic, doesn't it?)

As we considered this V Formation structure and the behavior of the birds, we were struck by the clear analogous similarities to a number of examples out of standard business vernacular that were being demonstrated:

1. Leadership focused on a crystal clear Mission Statement (i.e. the destination)

2. Team Members clear on and in agreement with the Mission

3. Members and Leaders sharing responsibilities and Empowered so as to adopt other roles as needed

4. Teamwork replacing "Management by fiat"

5. Support, Help and Encouragement keeping the Team on track and productive

6. A Team far more productive and efficient than the Individual Members would be on their own

7. The "V formation" structure and processes creating a uniformity and consistency that is easily replicated, tracked and measured

8. A "Language" (or Terminology) for the Project process that would be unique, universal and clearly understood

9. A "Project" with a "defined goal" (i.e. to reach a specific destination), thereby making the temporary nature of the activity clear and obvious and non-threatening, while dramatically reducing the stress of clashes of styles.

We divided this book into three sections:

In PART I we cover:
1. What <u>The V-Formation Method</u>™ is,
2. How it works, and
3. How it is implemented.

PART I serves as a textbook and "how to" manual for introducing <u>The V-Formation Method</u>™ into an organization.

PART II is, essentially, an example of <u>The V-Formation Method</u>™ in action. We have created an enterprise and a project and introduced numerous issues commonly encountered in the project process to show how <u>The V-Formation Method</u>™ might address those issues.

In EPILOGUE II we provide contact information, should the reader have any questions, issues, or feedback for the authors.

PART I

THE V-FORMATION METHOD™

SYSTEM

Part I – An Overview of <u>The V-Formation Method</u>™

Section I. "V" Also Stands for "Visionary"

Crystallizing the "Destination" with Visionary Life Principles

As Business Life Coaches, our interest is in the daily activities of the organizations with which we work. We are generally engaged to assist clients to find their way from where they are to some wished-for result. Most often the issues that have confounded them are based in the confusions that exist between various conflicting versions they have of the result they think they are seeking. In other words they are attempting to move forward without having a clearly defined and universally understood destination.

In our coaching we describe ourselves as "map makers" and "tour guides". First, as "map makers", we coach our clients in the process of structuring their visions and defining them with such crystal clarity that there can be no doubt, no confusion and no misunderstanding of desired goals. Then, as a "tour guide", we are able to lead them on journeys of exploration and discovery of options and alternatives and new learnings, always moving toward a known and clearly understood end result, "vision", true goal...the "destination". Even if an obstacle is encountered along the way, a clearly defined and understood destination always returns us to the right track.

The point is that a "map" is of no value if you don't know where you are going. And a "route" is meaningless without a destination.

We are also referred to as "Visionary Life Coaches". But this is basically the same thing. A "visionary" is one who has such a clear picture of the true mission that every thought and every action taken is geared to always move toward its achievement. Earlier we showed JFK's "vision statement". Let's look at it again:

"I believe that this nation should commit itself to achieving the goal, before this decade is out, of landing a man on the moon and returning him safely to the earth"

Can any statement be clearer than that? Is there anything missing? Can there be any misunderstanding? Everything else is mere details. This is, to us, as clear a statement of a "VISION" that there can be.

You often hear the term "Mission Statement" to describe an organization's goals. But a "mission" is more descriptive of the path than of the goal. We prefer the term "Vision Statement". The terms are used interchangeably, but a "vision" can be "seen" in the mind. It can spur an emotional response and inspire passions. A "vision" goes beyond a simple and usually meaningless" statement of the business obvious (e.g. "Our goal is to make money"). It suggests a deeper reason for existence...a TRUE purpose.

This is the mission of a "visionary life coach"... to guide a client to a clear and defined purpose that can, and should, be constantly referred to, as we tend to allow events of the moment to lead us off track. We will expand on this later when we discuss the concept we call "**ONE DEGREE OF DIVERGENCE**". This concept instructs us that even a slight, but uncorrected, movement off track from a goal can result in a significant divergence and, as the result, the complete missing of the desired destination. For an example, consider what would happen if a ship left London with a goal of sailing to New York. Should it divert even a single degree from its true heading, and not correct the divergence, what would happen? It may well end up in Rio de Janeiro instead.

And so it must be with a "Project".

A Project cannot begin without having a crystal clear Vision Statement of its true purpose. If the one seeking to create "Project A" has only a GENERAL idea of a goal or a desired end result, then perhaps there should FIRST be a project which has the crystal clear and singular purpose of creating a crystal clear Vision Statement for "Project A".

There can be no guessing. There can be no assumptions. There can be no terms with multiple possible meanings. There can be no goals without purposes, nor purposes without reasons understood by all.

Without a clear VISION the members of a Project Team could not know:

1. whether a picture shows a glass that is half full or half empty

2. whether a picture shows a golf ball that has stopped, or one that is still rolling toward the hole

3. whether a picture shows a sun that is rising, or one that is setting

4. whether every action taken by every member of the project team is, in fact, movement toward or away from the purpose of the project.

Yet, as we will learn, a VISION may possibly turn out to be unachievable due to reasons discovered during the journey to its attainment. After all, business is dynamic and circumstances change. This is not necessarily a bad thing. This result may save the organization from a substantial loss of time and effort and investment. But only PEOPLE can determine this outcome and make the decision to terminate or significantly alter a project. And this fact introduces another major concept which we call "**DYNAMIC FLUIDITY**".

"**Dynamic Fluidity**" is actually the subject of another topic in our series of "Lonely at the Top" publications for business leaders. Unlike "flexibility" which only means that something is capable of being bent or changed, "Dynamic Fluidity" instructs us that an organization is incapable of changing itself. An organization must conform to its existing rules of operation or there will be utter chaos. Thus we understand the term "sticking to the company line" to mean to follow the company "rules" until they are changed by people who have the authority to do so. Changes forced by intervening external or internal forces would always be negative or destructive. Only a person in an organization can introduce organized change in such a way as to make the change most positive and productive and responsive to the intervening force. "Dynamic Fluidity" is a characteristic of the most successful organizations, ones most alert to the existence of positive and negative influences and able to most swiftly react to circumstances, and ones who have nurtured visionary leadership skilled in addressing the realities of change and fluid business activity.

What <u>The V-Formation Method</u>™ Really Is

<u>The V-Formation Method</u>™ is a universal **PROJECT MANAGEMENT SYSTEM**.

It is "universal" because it is adaptable for use by <u>any</u> entity, group or organization of <u>any</u> kind and of <u>any</u> size and for <u>any</u> kind of project.

It is a "system" because it is a complete, uniform and consistent project management structure and process. There is nothing to add except the <u>Vision Statement</u> of the specific project itself. It is, in the vernacular, a "plug-n-play" infrastructure which, once in place, is immediately available to provide a structure and process for the planning, launching and management of any project.

As a complete "system":

1. Its structure, rules, and consistent terminology make its temporary nature obvious and non-threatening, greatly reducing the potential stress of clashes of management styles and executive levels (i.e. the "ruffling of feathers")

2. As a "plug-n-play" infrastructure, it provides a rapid method to introduce, launch, perform, wrap up, and analyze any project, from specific department applications to enterprise-wide tactical/strategic planning or process implementation.

3. All "surprises" are gone. Everyone knows what to expect. Everyone in the organization is trained to know how the system works. Everyone has the potential to lead. And everyone is ready to be "plugged in" to any project requiring their specific skills or knowledge. It makes projects fun, enjoyable and rewarding experiences because so that staff members look forward to being part of project teams.

4. It dramatically reduces project planning and organizing time because the uniform structure is always in place and ready to go, making all projects consistent in design, process, structure and procedures.

5. It makes collection, maintenance, access and analysis of performance and achievement metrics and project results uniform and relatable and comparable for future review and comparison or for utilization in future projects.

6. From management's perspective, uniformity in new project introductions results in the simplest and most consistent, efficient, productive and easily replicable processes and analytics.

Once an organization incorporates <u>The V-Formation Method</u>™ into its operation processes:

1. It will have created an infrastructure and platform for every project in the future.

2. It will have created trained and interchangeable staffs of project managers and team members ready to "plug in" to any future project assignments.

3. Future projects will focus on, encourage and reward teamwork, mutual support, cross training, cooperation and coordination.

4. Staff will realize personal development opportunities and will be exposed to other areas of the organization and realize a more profound understanding and appreciation of the work of others and the relationship of areas and departments to one another and to the whole of the organization.

Now let's move on to learn the Structure and Language of <u>The V-Formation Method</u>™.

Part I - An Overview of <u>The V-Formation Method™</u>

Section II. The "Language" of <u>The V-Formation Method™</u>

Why a Unique, Separate Terminology is so Critical

In the next section we will be covering how a V-Formation Project Structure is created, how it works and how it relieves the organization of the need to create new project structures, processes and procedures from scratch every time a new project is needed.

In this section we want to introduce the unique and fun "language" of <u>The V-Formation Method™</u>.

Throughout the Preface, Introduction, and Section I above, we repeatedly referenced the very real and potentially damaging physical and psychological disruptions a "project" can wreak on an organization.

These included:
1. Inexperienced project managers having to manage project team members who might even be their superiors in the organization

2. Project managers or their project sponsors who may not have the "ear" of organization decision makers and, therefore, have to struggle for the resources, time and budget needed for their project.

3. Project team members feeling disheartened and concerned about their existing jobs by being pulled from their "regular" jobs and thrown together in a group of a diversity of skills and temperaments and work styles

4. Emotions including fear, frustration and confusion creating an atmosphere less than conducive to maximum productivity or positive outcomes.

The more a project's format and processes emulate those of the organization's normal daily operations, the worse it is. This is because there appears to be nothing distinguishing, separating or differentiating the project, which we know is just a temporary activity, from the organization's core ongoing activities.

In other sections of this book, particularly in Section V. below which covers how to introduce The V-Formation Method™ to the staff, we discuss why the very success of The V-Formation Method™ is not only dependent upon the acceptance and support of top management, but also upon the clear and unwavering commitment and conveying of that support directly from top management to the rest of the staff.

It is imperative that the program be explained so that the relativity of project management to the V formation of migrating birds is clearly understood and that, to reinforce this connection, the program includes the "language of the birds". The language is then introduced...and the laughs begin. It becomes immediately and abundantly obvious that "projects" are separate activities with their own agendas, their own purposes, their own goals, their own temporary time frames...and that the relationship of the project team members to each other is NOT the same as the relationships of these same individuals in the normal operations of the organization.

The terminology we developed relates to "birds". Many titles are just for fun. But the effect is that a "vice president" is not being asked to appear subordinate to a "supervisor" if, in a particular project the "vice president" is an "uplifter" reporting to a "flight controller".

(At the end of the book we have provided a **"Glossary of Terms"** defining the "language of The V-Formation Method. Most of the terms and definitions are self-explanatory and many are mentioned in the next section which covers how the system works. Here we just want to highlight those terms necessary to understand the physical structure of the system.)

It all begins at the top!!!

Senior management cannot just delegate the introduction and implementation of The V-Formation Method system and walk away. It just won't work if they do. Just as with any other new application or process or operation, without the commitment, introduction and leadership from the very top, staff at all other levels will not take the program seriously or accept the program with the level of commitment to learning it, understanding it, accepting it, and following it necessary to its successful implementation and integration. Its many benefits will be lost and its very purpose will not be realized.

The first position to be filled by the organization is that of: **HEAD HONKER**. This is the "big bird" in the system, the individual who presides over the **TOP ECHELON** (i.e. the organization's V-Formation management team or steering committee), and the individual:
1. to whom all project requests are directed
2. who prioritizes all **FLIGHTS** (i.e. projects)

3. who assigns the **FLIGHT CONTROLLERS** (i.e. project managers)

4. to whom all **FLIGHT CONTROLLERS** report

5. who receives and maintains the records, details, results, performance data and measurement metrics from every completed **FLIGHT.**

6. who is the master of The V-Formation Method system and trainer and mentor of all **FLIGHT** participants.

The **HEAD HONKER** position is assigned by top management and reports to top management, and, depending on the size and structure of an organization, may be filled by the head or a delegated senior executive in the Project Management Office or Human Resources Department. In a smaller organization, the **HEAD HONKER** may be the president or small business owner or an engaged licensed **FLIGHT COACH** or consultant or the vice president of operations. In EVERY case, however, the position MUST be filled by a senior decision maker who either is a member of, or has the ear of, top management.

Again, depending on the size of the organization and its project requirements, the position of **HEAD HONKER** might be a part time activity or the full time activity of more than one individual.

The very first step in the process of preparing the **LAUNCH** of a new project is the creation of the project's **VISION STATEMENT** (i.e. its charter or true purpose) and its initial details which are contained in the project's **FLIGHT PLAN**. Initial drafts of these documents are created by the source, or sponsor, of the project request and may be modified a number of times once the **FLIGHT** has **LAUNCHED**.

The **HEAD HONKER**, either alone or in consultation with the source of the project request, chooses a **FLIGHT CONTROLLER** (i.e. Project Manager) with, if appropriate, the approval of the **FLIGHT CONTROLLER'S** superior.

The **HEAD HONKER** together with the **FLIGHT CONTROLLER**, and, if appropriate, the source of the project request, then must select the **UPLIFTERS** (i.e. the individual team members) who will constitute the **FLOCK** (i.e. the project team) of the **FLIGHT ECHELON** (i.e. the "V" formation of the project). The **FLOCK** is chosen based on an estimation of the requisite skills, knowledge and experience it is felt the project will require. It should be anticipated, however, that in virtually every case, in the course of the **ECHELON'S** journey toward its **DESTINATION**, determinations will be made that certain skills may not be required or that unexpected **HEADWINDS** may require other skills be added or departments not previously considered, might be effected and should be represented in the **FLOCK**.

Since the "V" of the **ECHELON** has two "wings", members of the **FLOCK** will be designated as **WING LEADERS** and will be responsible for leading parts of the **FLOCK** to address delegated components of the project's responsibilities.

To maintain ongoing notes and records of the **FLIGHT'S** activities and progress and its communications between the **FLIGHT** and the **HEAD HONKER**, a member of the **FLOCK** might be designated the **QUILL**, which is the **FLIGHT'S** secretary and record keeper.

At the end of the **FLIGHT**, either because it reached its **DESTINATION** or was prevented from doing so by encountering a **GOOSE DROPPING** (i.e. a fatal **FLIGHT**-ending event), the **HEAD HONKER**, or a committee designated for this purpose, might choose to award **GOLDEN EGG CERTIFICATES** or **QUILLIES** to members of the **FLIGHT FLOCK**.

And so it goes.....

Note how the unique language is both humorous and so removed from the lexicon of "business" as not to possibly be confused with standard business operation. The critical point, again, is that staff members who want to be considered for positions on future **FLIGHTS** must study the manual, learn how the system works, learn how to qualify for positions such as **WING LEADER** or **FLIGHT CONTROLLER**, learn how to earn **GOLDEN EGG CERTIFICATES** or **QUILLIES** (and whatever "bonuses" the organization decides to award), and learn and be able to utilize the "language" of the system

In the **Glossary of Terms** we added a number of definitions we thought were appropriate to maintain the levity of the program. Hopefully our point in doing so is clear. It is not requisite that every term be used, and we are certain that there are many cleverer people that will come up with any number of terms we didn't think of.

Organizations with large, divisible projects or multiple, simultaneous projects may introduce special awards to **FLOCKS** which, for example, reach their **DESTINATIONS** first, save the organization money, or which come in under budget (i.e. with **BIRD FEED** remaining), and so on.

(THE AUTHORS HAVE PROVIDED OUR CONTACT INFORMATION IN EPILOGUE II AND WOULD BE VERY GRATEFUL FOR EMAILS WITH SUGGESTIONS OF CONTESTS AND AWARDS AND TERMS WE MIGHT ADD TO GLOSSARIES IN FUTURE EDITIONS.)

Now let's move on to see how a V-Formation structure is added to an organization.

Part I – An Overview of <u>The V-Formation Method</u>™

Section III. Creating a V-Formation Method System

Letting <u>The V-Formation Method</u>™ do the Heavy Lifting

In Section I we learned what <u>The V-Formation Method</u>™ IS and what it contributes to an organization. In summary, it provides uniformity, simplicity and fun to the creation, launch and management of projects
which are, by definition, temporary, albeit critical, but usually both mundane and stressful interruptions of the normal daily activities of an organization.

In Section II we introduced the "language" of The V-Formation Method™. We discussed why it is so critical to maintain a separation of the entire project creation and management structure and operation from the normal day-to-day structure and operation of the rest of the enterprise. Having its own "language" is a major contributing component to accomplishing this.

Having a project management system always in place and ready to go, particularly one with which the staff is familiar, greatly accelerates the time it normally would take just to create a process and structure from scratch every time a new project was needed. Having a uniform process in place allows any adjustments or improvements to be instantly added and to immediately become parts of all future projects.

With the "wheel" in place, the organization does not have to spend time, energy, resources, and people power to "reinvent the wheel". This is the "heavy lifting" we are referring to. With The V-Formation Method™ system in place and trained staff prepared to immediately serve on Flight Teams and perform the
various functions, all that is needed is the project's Vision Statement and initial Flight Plan meetings to proceed.

The project is Launched quickly and progress is efficient and productive. Results are reported and maintained uniformly and are accessible to future project Flight Controllers who might take advantage of prior project's learnings and build on them. Use of time and resources is minimized. Projects are brought to faster and, often, more successful conclusions.

How The V-Formation Method™ Really Works

In Section II we introduced the "language" of The V-Formation Method™. A study of that section also provides a picture of how the system is structured. We discussed why one of the major psychological benefits of the system (and the way to have the most fun with it) is achieved by mandating that everyone participating in a **FLIGHT** must first study, master and utilize the "language" of the system.

The basic elements of any project are always the same and include:
1. the purpose of or reason for the project

2. the project team skills, knowledge and experience required
3. determinations of project team activities and deliverables
4. estimations of time, cost, budget, and required resources

Every organization has its own project approval process which must be followed so that only approved projects with clear and specific purposes (i.e. Vision Statements) are referred to the **HEAD HONKER** for **LAUNCH** preparation.

The **HEAD HONKER** is like the chairman of the board presiding over the organization's **TOP ECHELON**, the committee responsible for understanding the **VISION STATEMENT** of the organization itself so that it can determine priorities and relevance of approved projects to the goals of the enterprise, availabilities and best uses of resources and the initial preparatory steps and **FLIGHT FLOCK** assignments. The **TOP ECHELON** may also determine from its records of past **FLIGHTS** whether data already exists that might be utilized in a particular new project.

The **HEAD HONKER** AND the **TOP ECHELON** (i.e. "steering") committee are also responsible for gathering from interviews and on evaluation forms, upon completion of every **FLIGHT**, data on the performance of **FLIGHT CONTROLLERS**, **WING LEADERS**, and **UPLIFTERS**. They then determine rewards and the awarding of **GOLDEN EGG CERTIFICATES** and **QUILLIES** as they deem earned.

Collected information should include:
1. effectiveness in each role performed
2. leadership and delegation skills
3. support and encouragement of others (ability to "provide positive strokes" and "sooth ruffled feathers")
4. initiatives and commitment to the mission
5. attitude, contributions, teamwork

(From a personnel standpoint, a project, being a temporary activity, is an ideal learning opportunity for management to "test" perceived skills and abilities by empowering employees, allowing them opportunities to make mistakes and to learn from the mistakes, to note how they manage, nurture, support and encourage others, how they work toward the achievement of organization goals, and how they respond to cross-training and working on teams and to opportunities to multi-task and perform other functions.)

Now is a good time to refer back to the "science" of migrating birds where we listed significant observed behaviors, most notably:
1. that the leader was clear on the flight's destination so that every action and activity was viewed from the standpoint of how it contributed to moving the flight toward that destination...or brought the flight back if it strayed off the correct flight path.

2. that the birds were heard to always be encouraging each other to move forward and helping each other if one stumbled and needed assistance

3. that birds in the rear or the leaders in the front were most likely to tire fastest and would be allowed to move to the center of echelon wings to rest and regain strength, thus allowing other qualified birds to move into their roles of leadership or support.

4. that each bird received "uplift" from the bird in front and that this "support and teamwork" allowed the echelon to travel significantly further distances between **OASIS** stops than individual birds could have traveled on their own.

Note the obvious relativity of this behavior to the journey of a project team moving toward its project objective (i.e. destination).

Rarely does a **FLIGHT** go as originally planned. The ability of a **FLIGHT CONTROLLER** to make in-flight corrections when **HEADWINDS** are encountered may well determine when or whether the **FLIGHT** will reach its destination.

In the project planning phase a **FLIGHT PLAN** is created that establishes the details of the journey, mapping the path to the **FLIGHT'S DESTINATION**. It includes the scheduling of **OASES**, or scheduled meeting points where records are updated, activities and progress are reviewed, reports are provided where appropriate and adjustments are made. A **HEADWIND** is an unanticipated, unplanned obstacle that requires, at least, an unscheduled **OASIS** stop in order to assess the situation and determine how best to proceed.

It may be determined that representatives of other areas of the organization need to be brought in, even for the singular purpose of addressing singular issues. It may also be that a new **WING** needs to be added to the **FLIGHT**, coming off one of the existing **WINGS** and tasked with addressing a specialized area as an ongoing activity of the **FLIGHT**.

Specific tasks and activities are assigned to each **WING** and individuals **WING LEADERS** are assigned to lead each **WING**.

Sometimes an obstacle is so critical that it brings the **FLIGHT** to a complete and permanent halt. These fatal occurrences are called **GOOSE DROPPINGS** and are not necessarily bad happenings. It may be that the **FLIGHT**, during its journey, determined very good reasons why the **FLIGHT** should NOT continue. Perhaps there were miscalculations or misunderstandings of costs or of how other areas would be affected. This result may end up saving the organization significantly.

Again, we suggest a study of all of PART I with a concentration on learning and understanding the "language" in the Glossary...together with any additional words the organization adds to represent unique elements of its particular structure or industry.

In PART II we present an example, only partly fictional and drawn heavily from very real experiences of the authors, both as coaches and as senior executives, of <u>The V-Formation Method</u>™ System **in action**. We purposely complicate issues and add numerous intervening, disrupting, and unanticipated obstacles in order to demonstrate the flexibilities...or **DYNAMIC FLUIDITY**...that must be allowed to exist, both in the structure of the system and in the training and empowerment allowed the participating individuals, in order to rapidly and most effectively address these occurrences.

Part I – An Overview of <u>The V-Formation Method</u>

Section IV. "Behavior Style" Profiling of FLIGHT FLOCK Members

Birds of a Feather my Flock Together... but not Necessarily Work Well Together

"Birds of a Feather" are individuals with similar or identical thoughts and behaviors. When a staff consists of only "birds of a feather", serious problems may occur. They might all agree on something because they all think alike, but that "something" they all agree on might be wrong. (As a **FLOCK** on a Project **FLIGHT**, they may all agree to fly in a certain direction, but it may be the wrong direction.) Or, worse, they may not be able to agree on anything because they are all so analytical that they suffer from "paralysis by analysis" and can't make a decision.

On the other hand, a **FLOCK** of diversified behaviors might face conflicts created by that very diversity. For example, a quick decision maker, which we refer to as a "ready, fire, aim" personality, would certainly conflict with a slow, plodding fact gathering analytical type. Or picture a take-charge type who is expected to take orders from a consensus building team player type.

These are the common conflicts organizations face when a required diversity of skills places a diversity of personality or behavior "styles" on a project team.

Understanding one's own likes and dislikes and drivers, motivators and intimidators helps us to better understand how we behave and why we react and behave the way we do in different situations. If every individual in a group (such as a **FLIGHT** team) knew and understand both their own natural "behavior style" and that of the others with whom they are interacting, whether at work, home, school or socially, the better each individual would understand how best to deal with the others in order to accomplish the purpose of the relationship, from getting things done to just getting along.

Generally referred to as "personality tests", behavior profiles are not really "tests", nor are they about psychology, intelligence, skills or abilities. We are more comfortable referring to them as "personality profiles" or "behavior style profiles" since they create a picture of an individual's motivators and reactors.

There are basically two types of behavior. Our "natural" behavior style is who we really are, while our "adapted" style is the behavior we display that we believe is appropriate in individual situations. In other words, one is who we really are and the other is who we think we are supposed to be or who we want others to think we are. An example would be a quiet, meek and mild-mannered individual who feels compelled to act loud, tough and demanding supervising a department of shop workers in a manufacturing plant.

Health-threatening stress levels increase the more, consciously or unconsciously, we attempt to be different than who we actually are. To the extent that we can "be ourselves" all the time, the happier and healthier we will be…and probably the more successful we will be.

The more stress we are under, the more we revert to our natural styles (our real selves) from whatever adapted style we may be trying to appear to be to others.

In the authors' private practices, at the beginning of new client relationships, knowing our own "styles" and learning those of the new clients instructs us to how best work with them.

We have found two programs to be the most accurate and of greatest value for our coaching purposes:

Target Training International's studies of the <u>Four Dimensions of Normal Behavior</u> utilizes forms which involve choosing one of four words or phrases that the individual feels best describes themselves. Two charts are created. One is called Personal Interests, Attitudes and Values (or PIAV) and instructs us <u>WHY</u> we behave the way we do, what interests us and what motivates us. Their identification of FOUR Dimensions of Normal Behavior, or DISC, identifies <u>HOW</u> we behave, consciously or unconsciously, to achieve our PIAV goals. Their program is based on studies of observable behavior.

The Four basic behaviors they identify are:
1. **D**ominance
2. **I**nfluence
3. **S**teadiness
4. **C**ompliance

All of us contain elements of all four behaviors to varying degrees, but we would be referred to by the one for which we received the highest number. For example, one might be referred to as "a high D".

A master of the DISC program would learn what motivates "high D's", what do they like, what do they fear, what do they want, how do they generally make decisions.
1. D most wants Results and most fears Loss of Control
2. I most wants Interactivity and most fears Rejection of "self"

3. S most wants Stability and most fears Change
4. C most wants Process and most fears Rejection of their Work.

DISC is a terrific program but it is quite complex and should only be utilized by those trained in DISC analysis. There is another program, however, that is similar to DISC, but simpler to interpret and can accomplish the same goals for our purposes.

The PERSONALITY PLUS SYSTEM, described in the book, Personality Plus, written by Florence Littauer is very similar in format to the DISC system. It also has the individual choose from four choices the word they feel best describes themselves in each of a list of categories. The answers are tallied and, like DISC, the order of four personality profiles are determined:
1. Choleric (which is comparable to Dominance)
2. Sanguine (which is comparable to Influence)
3. Phlegmatic (which is comparable to Steadiness)
4. Melancholy (which is comparable to Compliance).

When used as part of The V-Formation Method in larger organizations, personality profiling might be a function of a trained member of the **HEAD HONKER'S** staff and be required before being permitted to serve on a V-Formation **FLIGHT FLOCK**. The organization would decide whether profile results would be shared with all **FLOCK** members or only with the **FLIGHT CONTROLLER** who would consider them when making activity assignments.

Actually, personality profiles should never be administered, nor their results revealed to anyone, without the express written approval of the profiled individuals. This is extremely confidential information and should be handled and maintained with great care not to violate its confidentiality.

When used properly, an individual who knows his or her own "style" and that of someone with whom they are interacting, will know how to most effectively present information and make requests and how best to react and respond to how presentations and requests are made to them.

The result is peace and harmony and teamwork and appreciation of others...and a clearer understanding of oneself.

Part I – An Overview of <u>The V-Formation Method</u>™

Section V. Launching The V-Formation Method™ System

Introducing <u>The V-Formation Method</u>™ to the Staff

By now all of the pieces of <u>The V-Formation Method</u>™ system are in place. Top management knows:
1. What it is,
2. How it relates to Project Management,
3. Its "language", and,
4. How it works.

AND TOP MANAGEMENT AGREES WITH AND IS COMMITTED TO SUPPORTING IT.

A **HEAD HONKER** and **TOP ECHELON** have been selected and trained.

(Perhaps a licensed and trained **FLIGHT COACH** has been engaged to train and initially support the **HEAD HONKER** and to help get the program launched.)

Supplies of forms, checklists, Leave the Nest Certificates, Golden Egg Certificates and Quilly trophies are in stock.

Templates of spreadsheets have been created as content folders in which to collect, maintain and catalog data for easy access and reference by later **FLIGHTS**.

Now there is only one thing more to do.....tell the staff about it.

And, in the spirit of fun and acceptance, we urge this be done with the maximum amount of time and refreshments and in a party atmosphere. A room (conference room, cafeteria, large office or, ideally, an off-sight meeting room) should be decorated with V-Formation themes...photos of geese and military planes in v-formation flight, bird pictures, bird shaped name tags, bird nest candy dishes and quill-shaped pens. Let the imagination take wing. The more and the sillier, the merrier and more memorable the event will be. Introduce the program with fun and bird-related take-aways (which will hopefully end up on desks).

In presenting the program, it is critical to very seriously explain the purpose of having The V-Formation Method template on top of all projects from now on. Discuss the issues common to project management and explain how this program addresses those issues. The staff needs to understand the purpose so as to recognize the underlying seriousness of project management issues and how to use the program to deal with them.

(Again, licensed **FLIGHT COACHES** are trained how to most powerfully and effectively introduce the program. Engaging one to assist the launch of the system is generally a very good idea.)

Whether the program is introduced by the most senior top management individual possible, or by a **FLIGHT COACH** or, or by the newly designated **HEAD HONKER** introduced by the most senior top management individual possible......**THE PROGRAM WON'T WORK UNLESS THE STAFF BELIEVES TOP MANAGEMENT REALLY BELIEVES IN IT AND WILL SUPPORT IT.**

Ideally, the presentation of the program and the initial activities over the subsequent days should include:

1. passing out copies of this book to every participant so they can review the concept and details and glossary

2. quizzes on the "language" which must be passed as a qualification for participation in **FLIGHTS**

3. asking for questions and providing a method for ongoing questions

4. discussing the awards and rewards

5. producing charts in "v" formation as part of the explanation of the program in action

6. introducing the **HEAD HONKER** and all of those who will be responsible for the operation and maintenance of the program.

Awards, Rewards and Archives

Many studies have shown that recognition beats mere money as a satisfier and motivator. Pats on the back, sometimes called "attaboys" and "attagirls" can make a person's day, week, month...or a whole year.

And so it is with The V-Formation Method™ System.

We have designed three awards, but there is always room for more.

As with words that might be added to the "language", the authors would very much appreciate emails with suggestions of other forms of recognition and reward that we can share with others in the future.

The three basic awards we use are:

1. **Leave the Nest Certificate** - for successful completion of training in <u>The V-Formation Method</u> and documented mastery of the "Language"

2. **Golden Egg Certificate** - for membership on a successful **FLIGHT FLOCK** team (remember that a **FLIGHT** might still be "successful" even if it encounters a **GOOSE DROPPING** which ends the journey, for good and valuable reasons. before reaching the intended destination.

3. **Quilly Trophy** - for outstanding contribution to the success of a **FLIGHT**, given to **FLIGHT CONTROLLERS**, **WING LEADERS** or **UPLIFTERS** for significant contributions or achievements. A Quilly is only awarded to individuals nominated by team members during the wrap-up activities, either on an evaluation form or during an interview. Quilly Trophies must be approved by the **HEAD HONKER**.

We anticipate we will soon be able to contract to acquire large supplies of forms, checklists, certificates and trophies so as to be able to make them very affordable and available to all. Please contact us if this would be of interest to you.

We suggest a complete review of all of Part I before moving on to Part II. Part II reads like a short story about a company that has identified major projects. It chooses to utilize <u>The V-Formation Method</u>™ System and is very happy it does, because the projects encounter all sorts of obstacles, issues and challenges (i.e. **HEADWINDS**) along its journey from **LAUNCH** to **DESTINATION**. Only the **DYNAMIC FLUIDITY** of <u>The V-Formation Method</u>™ system allows the projects to move forward to **ARRIVE** successfully.

(The story is only partially fictional. It is actually based on a combination of actual situations encountered by the authors.)

PART II

THE V-FORMATION METHOD™ IN ACTION

A Manufacturer Addresses an Issue

Part II - <u>The V-Formation Method™</u> in Action
A Manufacturer Addresses an Issue

Section I. Defining the "Flight" and Mapping The Flight Path
Creating a Crystal Clear Vision Statement
Limitations of Resources, Budget and Time

Bill, the President of Net-Cast Ventures, is a true visionary. He built this successful mid-size manufacturer from scratch. His employment philosophy of teamwork and empowerment and promotion from within and allowing employees to "fail" and learn by those mistakes, had resulted in an organization of individuals with deep mutual respect for each other, pride in their company and a desire for achievement. The company was an industry leader in innovations and design of widgets and was admired by all who had dealings with it. But...Bill was concerned that the company was approaching a plateau and needed to make changes before the competition caught up with it.

He called us in to discuss options for how he might proceed.

We are Visionary Business Life Coaches and the developers of <u>The V-Formation Method</u>™ project management system. We quickly recognized that Net-Cast Ventures was a perfect candidate for our programs. In "Visionary Business Life" coaching we work with companies as they move through the phases of a business' existence from inception, through growth and change in both its internal operations and employee relations and its external relationships with existing and potential customers, markets, suppliers, professionals and the communities in which it has locations or just does business. We are "outsiders looking in", so we bring fresh perspectives and decades of experience to assisting management in recognizing opportunities and overcoming obstacles by guiding them on journeys of exploration and discovery of options and possibilities for achieving clearly defined goals.

As with <u>The V-Formation Method</u>™, we begin new engagements by introducing tools, such collaborative tools as "brainstorming sessions", to first create Vision Statements, the crystal clear goals and true purposes that it is the mission of our engagement to accomplish.

Bill told us he had seen a product at a customer's location that was nothing short of amazing. It was an add-on feature that made widgets run longer, do more, and cost considerably less to operate. The customer was thrilled with the results he was realizing from a prototype he had agreed to test for the inventor. The add-on had been operating flawlessly for over a year and he was preparing to purchase more of them to add to his other widgets. Bill immediately sensed that, if he had access to that add-on, he would be able to build a widget that would incorporate the add-on and, he suspected, would even cost less to manufacture than his current products. There would be nothing like it in the widget industry. He knew the inventor of the add-on to be an industry expert and felt he could approach him to make a deal…if that was the right thing to do. He wanted to know how we would suggest he proceed.

After long discussions, it was clear that this was a major decision that would mean a great deal of hard work and investment with implications and impacts on virtually every area of the company. There would be a number of large and complex projects necessary in order to consider every aspect and every phase from decision to implementation.

He felt he clearly needed to implement <u>The V-Formation Method</u>™ project management system.

Interestingly, it occurred to us that studying whether and, if so, how to implement a V-Formation system in a company is, itself, a PROJECT that needs to be analyzed by utilizing the V-Formation system. This is a true conundrum. This is a true "cart before the horse/chicken before the egg" dilemma. We solved it the only logical way possible (and the way for all future new clients to approach implementation). In order to most quickly create the system, demonstrate top management's total support so necessary to achieve employee "buy in", and to get to the real issue of what to do about the widget add-on would require the following, most easily implemented steps:

1. When introducing <u>The V-Formation Method</u>™ to the staff, Bill would announce himself as "ACTING HEAD HONKER"

2. He would then introduce members of senior management, in this case the Vice Presidents of Sales, Operations, Human Resources, and Finance as the "ACTING TOP ECHELON"

3. He would tell the employees that the company would be embarking on studies of major potential new opportunities and that everyone would be given opportunities to participate in future **FLIGHTS** that would be **LAUNCHED** to study and, if decided to do so, to implement these new opportunities.

4. He would say that he was counting on them, as he always did, hinting that awards and rewards and a lot of fun would accompany the hard work.

5. He would tell them that he trusted them and would be learning along with them in the capacity of a **BIRD WATCHER**, sitting in at **OASIS** meetings, and observing and only contributing when asked.

6. With the help of the Human Resources staff, he would have copies of The V-Formation Method™, including the Glossary of Terms passed out to every employee, and announce there would be training meetings to teach the system to everyone. Those successfully completing training would graduate and be presented with a signed and framed **LEAVE THE NEST CERTIFICATE**, immediately qualifying them for participation in future **FLIGHT** opportunities.

And so... The V-Formation Method™ was implemented.

This still left three major projects to be immediately addressed:
1. to explore whether to secure the add-on invention at all and, if so, on what basis
2. if the add-on invention is secured, how to incorporate it in the existing widget products line, and,
3. how to launch the resulting new products.

These were clearly not simultaneous projects. Project 2 depended on the result of Project 1 and Project 3 depended on the result of
Project 2.

The **Vision Statement** for Project 1 was simple:

"Determine whether and, if so, on what basis, the company should attempt to acquire the widget add-on invention".

Bill (the **HEAD HONKER**) called a meeting of his senior management team (the **TOP ECHELON**) and the decision was made to proceed to create a **FLIGHT** for Project 1. The team adopted the **Vision Statement** and determined the budget and resources that it felt were appropriate and set a time frame for completion.

The next step would be for them to:
1. Select a **FLIGHT CONTROLLER**, and,
2. With the help of the FLIGHT CONTROLLER, select the members of the FLIGHT **FLOCK**.

Part II – The V-Formation Method™
In Action
A Manufacturer Addresses an Issue

Section II. Creating the Flight Flock
Head Honker assigns Flight Controller, Wing Leaders and Flock Uplifters

Time was of the essence. There was concern that competitors would soon learn about the extraordinary add-on invention, recognize its potential and either beat Net-Cast Ventures to the acquisition or drive up the cost to acquire it. They agreed they needed to move quickly, so they set a time target of complete this project in four weeks.

Since this project would clearly touch every department in the company, the **TOP ECHELON** team decided that the **FLIGHT CONTROLLER** should be someone familiar with the whole operation. Bill asked the Vice President of Operations to assume this position, and he readily agreed.

With the **FLIGHT CONTROLLER** in place, discussions turned to the structure of the V-Formation itself. The team felt that they needed two areas of global input: sales/marketing potential and manufacturing.

It was decided that the Vice President of Marketing should be **WING LEADER 1** of a wing focused on studying the sales and marketing issues and potentials. This wing would include sales, marketing and customer service **UPLIFTERS** with as much customer and general industry knowledge as available.

For **WING LEADER 2** they selected the Plant Manager of the local facility. He had significant years manufacturing experience in the widget industry. His wing would be responsible to globally assess the engineering, manufacturing, and distribution issues and would consist of **UPLIFTERS** selected from these areas.

This project was going to test The <u>V-Formation Method</u>™ and was dealing with a topic of major importance to the future of the company. In order to keep to his philosophy of trusting and empowering his people and, at the same time, to stay significantly involved, Bill announced his decision to assume the role of **BIRD WATCHER** so everyone would know he might sit in on meetings just to observe how everything was moving forward. Given Bill's history with his employees, it was not surprising that no one had a problem with this.

UPLIFTERS
National Sales Manager
Customer Service Director

WING LEADER 1
Vice President of Marketing

FLIGHT CONTROLLER
Vice President of Operations

WING LEADER 2
Plant Manager

UPLIFTERS
Chief Product Engineer
Assembly Line Supervisor

Part II – <u>The V-Formation Method</u> In Action

A Manufacturer Addresses an Issue

Section III. Mapping Scheduled Oases Planning Meetings and Interim Reporting

We were really impressed. It had only been three weeks since Bill had engaged us to implement <u>The V-Formation Method</u> in Net-Cast Ventures, introduce it to the staff, and create and staff the **FLOCK** for **FLIGHT 1**, the project to determine whether to try to acquire the widget add-on invention and, if so, on what basis to try to do so. Clearly Bill and his senior staff were committed.

Several steps had actually taken place simultaneously. While Bill and his senior executives were meeting to discuss the project, deciding to move forward with it and selecting the **FLIGHT CONTROLLER**, we took on the task of preparing <u>The V-Formation Method</u> Introductory Event (the "**LAUNCH**").

Years ago, the company had created a recreation room near the employee cafeteria where employees could take breaks and rest on comfortable chairs and couches. They could watch television, play video games, read or have snacks. This was a large room which could also be set up with chairs and tables for programs during lunch.

This was the setting for the **LAUNCH** Event. With the help of a local printer and some very creative and artistic Net-Cast Ventures employees, the room was decorated with appropriate themes: blue skies with fluffy clouds around the walls, geese taking off and landing, name tags shaped like birds, pens with feathers so they looked like quills, and so on.

Because Net-Cast Ventures has four national locations, the managers of the other three locations were brought in to participate in the presentation at corporate headquarters. They would then hold similar events for the staffs at their own locations. Bill promised to attend each of these events to demonstrate the commitment and support of top management for this new system.

We were also asked to attend these events and, at each one, we were introduced as the **FLIGHT COACHES** who would be available to train and support the local representatives assigned to the **HEAD HONKER's TOP ECHELON** team.

So **FLIGHT** 1 was ready for **LAUNCH**. The first meeting of the ECHELON team was an open discussion to develop a **FLOCK** consensus on the details of how best to proceed. At this and at every meeting the Vision Statement was read and a short discussion held to determine that the **FLIGHT** was still on track toward its clear **DESTINATION**.

It was decided that it was important that this **FLIGHT** not get sidetracked by running into **HEADWINDS**, obstacles in this case consisting of getting stuck in a quagmire of more details than were this team's mandate. Theirs was a "50,000 foot overview" mission intended only to conclude with two recommendations:

1. whether the company should try to acquire the widget add-on, and

2. if so, on what basis.

They had four weeks to reach their **DESTINATION** and report back to Bill in his capacity as **ACTING HEAD HONKER**. The decision was made to assign tasks to each **WING,** to hold ten minute daily status meetings, and to "land" every Friday for an **OASIS** rest in order to review the week's progress in terms of the Vision Statement, make decisions about next steps...and to wish each other a good weekend.

As is the case with virtually every V-Formation Method utilization, **confidentiality** is assumed. The matters involved are always internal to the organization and therefore, by their very nature, are secret. In the case of **FLIGHT 1**, confidentiality was even more critical, so the **ECHELON** team agreed that no discussion of the nature or content or activities of this **FLIGHT** would be shared with anyone other than Bill who would then discuss them with his **TOP ECHELON** team. It was further agreed that, if any **FLOCK** member felt that other areas of expertise were needed, they would first bring this need to the **FLIGHT CONTROLLER** who, if he felt the need, could call for an unscheduled **OASIS** rest at any time to discuss the issue.

Activity assignments were made at this first **PRE-LAUNCH** meeting. **WING 1** would address the sales and marketing potential of the widget add-on and **WING 2** would focus on issues of engineering, manufacture, distribution and incorporation into existing product lines.

And Bill would make contact with the inventor of the widget add-on to begin the most exploratory conversations about the inventor's desires for moving his invention to market.

Week One would primarily consist of fact gathering.

They were ready to **LAUNCH** the **FLIGHT**.

Part II - <u>The V-Formation Method</u>
In Action
A Manufacturer Addresses an Issue

Section IV. Launching the Flight

The **ECHELON** took off and quickly went to work. The first week involved a lot of planning.

WING 1 developed lists of data needs:
1. demographics and geographics of likely markets
2. relation of the add-on to existing products on the market
3. projections of possible sales levels.

WING 2 worked on issues of production and distribution such as:
1. equipment additions
2. personnel requirements
3. technology upgrades
4. output projections
5. areas of possible obstacles.

But everyone realized that all of this would be meaningless if Bill was not able to bring back some hopeful news about his efforts to engage with the inventor.

So, when Friday of the first week rolled around, the **FLIGHT** landed for its first scheduled **OASIS** rest with great anticipation and excitement.

And Bill did not let them down. Knowing how critical it was that he bring in good news about the inventor, he went first and announced that the inventor had been pleasantly surprised to hear from him, as the inventor had actually planned to contact Bill for the same purpose of exploring whether there might be a fit between them. Just as Bill's executive team, based on their collective decades of experience in the widget industry, had intuitively sensed a strong fit, the inventor himself, with his extensive knowledge of the business, had sensed that Net-Cast Ventures was the perfect fit for him as well. Bill and the inventor had spoken twice that week and had had substantive conversations about possible directions. The inventor, whether he felt a need to stay connected to his "baby" or just because he wanted to follow it into the market, did not want to sell the add-on. He wanted to license its production. Bill felt this was certainly a viable approach as it would accomplish his two goals of: 1. controlling the add-on and 2. having exclusive rights to its production and sale. Bill also wanted to take advantage of the inventor's vast knowledge and had introduced the possibility of him joining Net-Cast Ventures for some period of time as a consultant.

The team was ecstatic. This was great news. It meant they could move forward with what, in effect, was really a "due diligence" mission. They still recognized the need for some speed to head off the possibility of a competitor coming into the picture.

WING LEADER 1 and WING LEADER 2 both asked to be able to bring some additional expertise into the FLOCK. Sales and Marketing wanted the input of some of its most seasoned field representatives as they new the customers and the competitors better than anyone. Plant and Production just wanted some technology advice to be sure they weren't overlooking areas of significant costs of time and investment. The FLIGHT CONTROLLER reported these requests to the TOP ECHELON team and the HEAD HONKER (who, at this point, was still Bill). Several long time and trusted employees were approved and were brought onto the ECHELON.

The next Monday, the ECHELON took off again to continue the FLIGHT.

Over the next two weeks facts were gathered and projections calculated. Bill and the inventor stayed in communication, each suggesting possibilities for how their relationship might look and what elements might or might not be negotiable.

Bill and the inventor both felt a tangible "thank you" was owed to the customer who, as both a significant purchaser and user of Net-Cast Venture widgets and as a friend and one-time colleague of the inventor had agreed to serve as a "beta sight" for the testing of the add-on, had brought them together.

Part II - <u>The V-Formation Method</u>
In Action
A Manufacturer Addresses an Issue

Section V. Dealing with "Headwinds" and "Goose Droppings"
Addressing Unanticipated Issues
Unscheduled Oases

A **"HEADWIND"** is an obstacle to be overcome in what would otherwise be a smooth journey. It is a very rare journey that never encounters an obstacle, or, in fact, many of them. Treated properly, **HEADWINDS** can serve as learning experiences, alerting a **FLIGHT** to the existence of such obstacles, and allowing the **FLOCK** to prepare to deal with them.

The Net-Cast Venture **FLIGHT** had anticipated and thereby avoided one **HEADWIND** by understanding its true mission and purpose to be an overview. They thus avoided getting bogged down in a myriad of micro-detail. By anticipating and avoiding this **HEADWIND**, the **FLIGHT** was able to maintain its timeline schedule.

A **"GOOSE DROPPING"** is more significant than a mere **"HEADWIND"**. It is, in fact, a obstacle that can't be overcome and, therefore, is fatal to the mission. It terminates the **FLIGHT** before it can reach its **DESTINATION**.

A **GOOSE DROPPING** is not necessarily a bad thing. It, too, is a learning opportunity that could easily save a company from significant losses by saving the company from proceeding with actions that could result in significant damage to the business.

Fortunately for Net-Cast Ventures, **FLIGHT 1** went smoothly. The **FLOCK** continuously reviewed its mission and brainstormed lists of possible **HEADWINDS** and **GOOSE DROPPINGS**. This both kept them alert to possible obstacles and allowed them to prepare actions to overcome them in advance of actually encountering them. They recognized that encountering a fatal **GOOSE DROPPING** would still be within the definition of their Vision Statement and, although it would end the **FLIGHT**, it would do so for very right reasons.

(Another definition of a **GOOSE DROPPING** describes when a single, but critical, member of a **FLIGHT** is unable for any reason to continue with the **FLIGHT** and, as a result, the **FLIGHT** has to terminate without reaching its **DESTINATION**. In the case of Net-Cast Ventures, although the inventor of the widget add-on technically was not a member of the **FLOCK**, his involvement in the process was clearly critical. Had he dropped out of negotiations for whatever reason, this would have been tantamount to a **GOOSE DROPPING** out of the sky, bringing down the entire **FLIGHT**.)

Some of the obstacles the **FLOCK** considered included:
1. Bill being unable to reach agreement with the Inventor
2. The widget add-on not working as all thought it would
3. The widget add-on not being compatible with Net-Cast Venture's entire product line
4. Production equipment, parts or other requisite technology not being cost effective or not available at all
5. Costs exceeding expectations, making the add-on not financially viable or profit margins adequate
6. The potential markets not being of sufficient size or having sufficient interest to support the production investment
7. The add-on having unanticipated competition from unanticipated sources

Over the remaining weeks, each time a **WING** felt it might be encountering a **HEADWIND**, the **FLOCK** would land for an unscheduled **OASIS** rest stop meeting to address the situation. By re-directing efforts, changing assignment priorities, bringing in additional members just to address specific issues, they were successful in overcoming every **HEADWIND**. They reached their **DESTINATION** successfully and on time.

Part II – <u>The V-Formation Method</u>
In Action
A Manufacturer Addresses an Issue

Section VI. Arriving at the Flight's
Destination
Final Reports to the Head Honker

And so, with "high fives" all around, Net-Cast Venture's **FLIGHT 1** landed at its **DESTINATION.**

The **FLOCK'S** final **OASIS** rest stop was used to collect and collate the data results, assemble reports, and conduct a final review of recommendations for presentation to the **HEAD HONKER** and the **TOP ECHELON.**

Most commonly, a **FLIGHT** would end with the **FLIGHT CONTROLLER** presenting a final report to the **HEAD HONKER** <u>in writing </u>and in the format adopted by the company to assure uniformity and ready accessibility of its material to others in the future.

This Net-Cast Venture **FLIGHT** had the mission purpose of having to recommend whether and, if so, how, to proceed with the acquisition of the widget add-on. It was decided that the importance and urgency of this mission was so sensitive and critical, and in order to be available to answer questions, a written <u>and oral</u> presentation should be made by the entire **FLOCK** to the senior executive committee which, in this case, happened to also be the **TOP ECHELON**.

In regard to this project, Bill had worn a number of feathers. He was:
1. the requester/originator of the project
2. the acting HEAD HONKER
3. the BIRD WATCHER
4. the most senior supporting executive.

WING LEADER 2, on behalf of his WING which included representation from production, engineering, plant operations, distribution and finance, reported that:
1. They found that the simplicity of design of the widget add-on resulted in an acceptably low cost of production.

2. The add-on could easily be adapted to Net-Cast Venture's entire widget line.

3. Because of the simplicity of attachment, the add-on could be manufactured as a retrofit to virtually every widget, REGARDLESS OF MANUFACTURER, currently in the field.

4. The size and weight of the add-on made storage, shipment and distribution easily cost effective.

WING LEADER 1, on behalf of his WING which included sales, marketing, and finance was equally optimistic. Their analysis of demographics, markets and geographics had concluded that:

1. The widget add-on was compatible and easily added to the company product line as a stand alone product, an add-on option to the widget line, an integrated component of a new line of widgets, or as a component sold to other manufacturers as an OEM (Original Equipment Manufacturer) product.

2. With the add-on's adaptability, it not only served existing general markets as a retrofit add-on to widgets already in the field, but it also opened coveted new markets, especially the coveted automotive market.

3. Marketing also saw major new opportunities in international markets.

4. Sales projected additional new sales potentials by the Year Five in the hundreds of units per year, producing millions of dollars of additional revenues.

The final recommendation of the **FLIGHT** team was obvious:

1. acquire the widget add-on either by outright purchase or exclusive license, and,

2. secure the services of the inventor as a consultant for a period of time, as his reputation and knowledge would add manufacturing expertise to production and credibility to marketing.

Part II – <u>The V-Formation Method</u>
In Action
A Manufacturer Addresses an Issue

Section VII. Awarding Golden Eggs
And Quillies
Wrapping up the Project

How an organization chooses to "wrap up" a project may depend on a number of variables including, perhaps, the size of the organization or whether the project had enterprise-wide significance or just effected a single department.

In EVERY case, however, organization-wide recognition must be given in order for the staff to be continuously aware of <u>The V-Formation Method</u> ™system. Framed certificates, trophies, or any other form of physical recognition that would hang on a wall or sit on a desk would serve as a reminder "attaboy" or "attagirl" pat on the back to the recipient of management's recognition and appreciation of a contribution or an accomplishment.

Bill, for himself and for the entire senior management team, expressed his profound gratitude to the **FLIGHT 1 FLOCK** for the outstanding job they had done. He personally met with and thanked each member individually and promised to let them know the final resolution of the quest for the widget add-on. He privately planned to honor them in a public, company-wide event should, hopefully, he be successful in securing the exclusive rights to the widget add-on.

.....WHICH, IN FACT, HE WAS!

Shortly after the **FLOCK'S** "Wrap Up" meeting with Bill (the **HEAD HONKER**) and the senior management team (the **TOP ECHELON**), Bill contacted the inventor. Serious negotiations went on for several months, but did conclude with Net-Cast Ventures securing exclusive rights to the manufacture and sale of the widget add-on. The Inventor agreed to a multi-year consulting agreement that would engage him to train and work with sales, marketing and production and to represent Net-Cast Ventures at customer presentations and trade shows. The inventor was very pleased with the ongoing royalties agreement that continued on after the consulting engagement wound down and expired.

After the agreements were signed and the inventor was on board, Bill shared with him the final reports of the **FLIGHT 1** project. This excited the inventor even more, as the potential for more sales and more markets meant more royalties and the potential appeared substantially greater than even he had thought.

So it made sense to hold an event at corporate headquarters and smaller versions at the other Net-Cast Venture locations that both honored and awarded the **FLOCK** of **FLIGHT 1** and introduced the inventor and the new product.

In his meetings with the individual **FLOCK** members, Bill had casually asked each individual about the contributions of other members, including reference to management styles and teamwork. He realized that The V-Formation Method was, in addition to all of its other attributes, a great way to "test" potential rising stars in the organization by offering them opportunities in the temporary world of a "project". If a performance were less than stellar, the ending of the project would make career-damaging moves unnecessary. The employee would merely return to his or her regular position. There would be no "demotion". The company could then assess where the individual needed training, quietly provide it and later provide another "project" opportunity to assess improvement.

At the award event, Bill announced the name of each **FLOCK** member to the gathered staff, called each individual forward and provided each with a signed and framed **GOLDEN EGG CERTIFICATE** acknowledging his or her participation and contribution to the successful **FLIGHT**.

With an eye to keeping the future "club" of **QUILLY** recipients small and exclusive, he chose to present only one **QUILLY** trophy to the **FLIGHT CONTROLLER** for his outstanding efforts in leading the first ever V-Formation Method **FLIGHT** to its **DESTINATION** and to the highly successful achievement of its <u>Vision Statement</u>.

We had advised Bill to use the occasion of this event to emphasize how <u>The V-Formation Method</u> system had worked, how they now had the beginnings of an archive of uniform documents of the accomplishments of **FLIGHTS**, which documents would be readily available to save others in the future from having to "reinvent" any wheels.

He also agreed with our suggestion that he announce the formation of a great number of **FLIGHT** opportunities that would be created around the incorporation, manufacture, sale, distribution, and service of the extensive new line of products and services that the acquisition of the widget add-on had brought to Net-Cast Ventures.

Again, this case study is largely a true story, but we did incorporate some additional features to further our purpose of providing a very simple example of The V-Formation Method in action. Organizations choosing to implement The V-Formation Method on their own can easily just "practice" with simple small projects. They should always feel free to incorporate their own ideas for adding fun and additional value to the program.

If initial projects are more complex and involve multiple disciplines and departments, they may want to consider engaging the services of a Licensed and Trained Business Life **FLIGHT COACH** for all or part of the implementation and training aspects.

Since this book is about The V-Formation Method universal project management system and not really about a manufacturing business, what happened next at Net-Cast Ventures is not significant to our message. We do understand, however, that many readers may wonder what, in fact, did happen next, so we have created **EPILOGUE I** highlighting some of what occurred in what is actually an ongoing process at the company to this day.

THE V-FORMATION METHOD ™

EPILOGUE I
Case Study Wrap Up

EPILOGUE II
An Offer from the Authors

EPILOGUE I

Case Study Wrap Up

When business at Net-Cast Ventures got back to "normal", Bill turned over the **HEAD HONKER** function to the Human Resources Director who has, in turn, made <u>The V-Formation Method</u> system the primary structure of the Project Management Office. The Director of that office is now the **HEAD HONKER** and her staff constitutes the basic **TOP ECHELON**. It has become company practice, when a new project is approved, to add either the project requester/originator, or a member of the requester's staff, to serve on the **TOP ECHELON** during review meetings of that **FLIGHT'S** progress.

It has also become common practice to try to expose as many employees as possible to **FLIGHT** opportunities and assign them specific tasks and "management" positions. This has become a major component of Net-Cast Venture's internal training. It allows them the ability to expose and observe employee's growth without putting whole careers in jeopardy by forcing termination or demotion situations.

The company is really having fun with The V-Formation Method program, creating migrating bird themes whenever possible. They've had their marketing specialties provider design and create **LEAVE THE NEST** and **GOLDEN EGG** certificate forms with clouds and flying bird formations in the border and as a logo.

For a "**QUILLY**" trophy, they have designed a wooden piece consisting of three hamburger bun shaped circles of narrowing size to represent an ink well. Then they added a feather coming out the top to represent a quill. A flat space in the front of the circles is the location of a small engraved plaque showing the name of the individual, the name and date of the **FLIGHT** and words such as: "for outstanding contribution" or "outstanding leadership".

As for the widget add-on, incorporating it into the company line of products and services was a complex undertaking. Numerous **FLIGHTS** and WINGS coming off of **FLIGHT WINGS** (i.e. sub-committees) had to be created. Some involved enterprise-wide matters and others were internal to individual departments. Decisions had to be made in Sales, Marketing, Manufacturing and Information Technology.

In a brilliant move that has sent waves of excitement throughout the organization because of its implications for others, the plant production manager who had served as **WING LEADER 2** on **FLIGHT 1**, was promoted, with great fanfare, to the position of enterprise-wide Widget Add-on Product Manager with overall responsibility as its "product champion" for product use and development.

To date, <u>The V-Formation Method</u> project FLIGHTS have resulted in, to name just a few:

* Sales developing a new "hot line" quick response telephone system for handling customer inquiries about the widget add-on.

* Production developing a separate manufacturing area with 3rd shift capability.

* Factory electricians submitting and receiving approval for the design of new machine controls that significantly reduce production times

* A group of Plant Supervisors coming up with designs for progressive fixtures which speed the manufacturing process without requiring the purchase of new tooling. Currently, engineering has been asked to create drawings for the Supervisors' sketches.

* Quality Control devising and writing new protocols for product testing at critical phases of production.

* Engineering, working with Shipping, designing a reusable shipment container for product delivery to regular OEM customers.

As became obvious to everyone, in projects following The V-Formation Method™ universal project management system:

1. Leadership focused on a crystal clear Mission Statement (i.e. the destination)

2. Team Members were clear on the Mission

3. Members and Leaders were Cross-Trained and Empowered so as to adopt other roles as needed

4. Teamwork replaced "Management by fiat"

5. Support, Help and Encouragement kept the Team on track and productive

6. Teams were far more productive and efficient than the Individual Members would have been on their own

7. The "V formation" structure and processes created a uniformity and consistency that is easily replicated, tracked and measured

8. A "Language" (or Terminology) for the Project process that was unique, universal and clearly understood

9. A "Project" with a "defined goal" (i.e. to reach a specific destination), thereby made the temporary nature of the activity clear and obvious and non-threatening, while dramatically reducing the stress of clashes of styles.

And, in practice, produced:

10. Joy of accomplishment and achievement and reward

11. Fun and teamwork and support and friendly competition

12. MAJOR CONTRIBUTIONS OF GREAT VALUE TO THE ORGANIZATION.

EPILOGUE II

An Offer from the Authors

Yes...<u>The V Formation Method</u>™ does work. We know because we used it to create "**The V-Formation Method™**"...and to write this book.

1. We defined the project's "**Vision Statement**".
2. We shared and alternated in the roles of **Flight Controller** and **Uplifter**
3. We added sub-**Echelons** when needed to research or expand individual components
4. We established specific **Oases,** where we stopped to review progress and discuss issues to be certain we had not strayed the "one degree of separation".

5. We documented our results for analysis and reference for future iterations and program modifications.

6. And we were so pleased with ourselves....that, when we **Arrived** at our **Destination**, we awarded ourselves **Quillies**.

One of our principal goals was to write a book that would so clearly document the steps to creation of a **V-Formation Method Program** in any organization that the organizations could easily implement the Program entirely on their own. Simultaneously, we have begun locating and training selected business, life and leadership coaches around the country as **LICENSED V-FORMATION FLIGHT COACHES** able to provide training and ongoing and follow up support to client organizations.

Although this book does contain all of the information an organization, from a small group to a large enterprise, needs to know to learn and employ <u>The V-FORMATION METHOD</u>™, an enterprise might choose to engage the services of a trained and licensed **V-FORMATION FLIGHT COACH** to perform any or all of the following functions:

1. Train the assigned V-Formation Head Honker and Flight Controller(s)

2. Explain <u>The V-Formation Method</u>™ to enterprise management

3. Introduce <u>The V-Formation Method</u>™ to the staff for the first time

4. Assist in the development and oversight of initial projects

5. Be available, as needed, to assist the V-Formation Head Honker at any stage and for a contracted period of time.

If you have any issues or questions you would like to discuss with us as a client organization... or to learn more about the **licensed V-Formation Flight Coach Program**, please contact the authors at: **flightcoach@v-formationmethod.com** .

THE V-FORMATION METHOD™

APPENDIX:
Glossary of Terms

GLOSSARY OF TERMS

The "Language" of <u>The V-Formation Method</u>™

Arrival - completion of project mission (arrival at mission **Destination**)

Birds of a Feather - **Flock** members with similar or identical behavior/work styles

Bird Feed - another word for "budget" or "resources"

Bird Watcher - an individual asked or assigned to merely observe a Flight and assist or provide input to the Flight Controller as/when needed

Chart: plans, goals, steps, status updates - posted and continuously updated

Destination - Goal, Mission, True Purpose, "vision" of **Flight**

Echelon - "V"-shaped formation of the **Flock** assigned to a specific **Flight**

Echelon Planning and Status Evaluation Meetings - scheduled series of meetings from **LAUNCH** (inception) to **ARRIVAL** (completion) of mission

Flight – a specific project

Flight Coach - a trained, experienced business life coach who is licensed and authorized to be engaged by client organizations to
teach, train, mentor, support, and back up the client's **Head Honker** in introducing, implementing and integrating The V-Formation Method in the organization

Flight Controller - Flight Echelon Leader - ACTING leader of a specific Flight

Flight Echelon - Team assigned to a specific project

Flight Echelon Destination - defined mission/goal of specific **Flight**

Flight Echelon Destination Arrival Date - estimated or assigned completion date

Flight Plan - Where the Vision Statement concisely states the true purpose and goal of a project, the **Flight Plan** fills in the details of the mission and the specific steps of the journey toward achievement of the vision.

Flock - the project team members of a specific **Flight**

Golden Egg and Leave the Nest Certificate - certificates of involvement in and training presented to individual **Flight Flock** members upon completion of a **Flight**

Goose Droppings - a fatal **Flight**-ending event, realization or discovery that terminates the **Flight** and ends the project before reaching its **Destination**

Head Honker - Top Echelon Leader -"point person" - Organization's assigned senior manager of <u>The V-Formation Method</u> program and person to whom all **Flight Controllers** report

Headwind - obstacles and issues causing unscheduled **Oasis** stops that must be addressed before **Flight** can resume

Launch - inception of a specific **Flight**

Oasis - "resting points" - scheduled and unscheduled stops for planning, and evaluation meetings or reporting points along the path/journey to ARRIVAL

Quill - the member of a **Flock** assigned as secretary and record keeper for the **Flight**

Quillie - statuette/trophy presented to successful **Flight Controllers** or individuals making significant contribution to the success of a **Flight**

Ripple Effect - When geese land on lake, a ripple expands across the water. The actions and decisions of a Flight may effect many other departments

The Golden Egg(s) and "Quillies" - prizes, certificates, trophies to team members upon successful completion of targeted missions (i.e. arrival at an **Oasis**) and upon successful arrival at mission **Destination**

Top Echelon - Organization's V-Formation Management Team

Top Echelon Destination - defined missions/goals of organization

Top Echelon Destination Arrival Date - estimated or assigned completion date of a specific **Flight**

Uplifter 1 - member of V-Formation **Flock** and able to step in as a **Wing Leader**

Uplifter 2 - member of V-Formation **Flock**

V-Formation - "V" stands for the shape of the efficient, powerful and incredibly productive flight formation of migratory birds. In our use it also stands for "Visionary". . A "visionary formation" injects visionary business life principles into your projects, providing them with a crystal clear Mission and Destination....and then launching the journey to reach that vision and goal

Vision Statement - A **Flight's** mission, true purpose, goal, **Destination** created by visionary business life principles and formatted as a crystal clear vision understood by the **Flock**

Wing Leader 1 - leader of one wing of an **Echelon** and able to step in as **Flight Controller**

Wing Leader 2 - leader of one wing of an **Echelon** and able to step in as **Flight Controller**

www.ingramcontent.com/pod-product-compliance
Lightning Source LLC
Chambersburg PA
CBHW030842210326
41521CB00025B/823